Imagination
and feelings

written by Tracy Ford
illustrated by Diana Stransky

Note to parents:

This is intended to be an
interactive book.
Please have paper and something to write
or draw with close by. After each emotion, there
are questions to explore with your child. The
intention is to encourage vivid images and ideas
that will hopefully inspire creativity as well as
give comfort.

with love to:
Ranier and Autumn

Text copyright 2018 by Tracy Ford. Illustrations copyright 2018 by Diana Stransky. All rights reserved, including the right of reproduction in whole or in part in any form.

There are many ways to think about the things going on around you. One way is to use your imagination. It may not change what is happening, but it can change the way you *feel* about what is happening.

Sometimes I get scared.

Then I imagine being in a warm, safe place, with friends all around me.

What cozy, warm, place would you like to be in, if you were scared?

What would make that place feel even better?

Who would be with you?

Would there be magical creatures?

Would there be animals?

What colors or patterns do you see?

Is there a nice smell you like that could surround you?

What other wonderful things would be there?

Can you draw a picture of your special place?

Sometimes I get angry.

Then I imagine being in a place that makes me feel calm.

What calms you down?

Where would you be?

Who would be with you?

What would the weather be like?

How would it feel?

What would make you feel even more calm...

an animal?

a friend?

a magical creature?

What would you be doing?

Would you like to paint the image you see in your mind?

Sometimes I get frustrated.

Then I imagine that nothing can keep me from soaring to new heights.

What makes you feel frustrated?

What does it feel like?

What do you do when you are frustrated?

What color would your frustration be?

What sound would your frustration make?

Can you picture your frustration as a little creature that wants to help you?

Can you and this cute creature work together and figure out a plan for success?

Can you walk through some steps, one by one, until you see yourself succeeding?

Would it help to imagine the steps if you dance or sing or draw?

Sometimes I get lonely.

Then I imagine doing something that makes me feel good and warms my heart.

What warms your heart?

If you could do anything to help others, what would it be?

Where would you be?

Would anyone be with you?

What would your surroundings look like?

Can you imagine what it would feel like to help others in need?

Do you think you would still feel lonely?

What other things could you do to feel happy and content?

Can you paint or draw a picture of yourself being super happy?

Sometimes I get sad.

Then I imagine doing something amazing.

Is there something amazing you would like to do?

Would you fly, be invisible, talk to animals, or just be an awesome person?

Where would you like to be?

What would the weather be like?

Would anyone, or anything, be with you?

What would it feel like?

Can you describe the colors and sounds around you?

Can you describe the scene?

Do you want to write a poem or song about what you see, or maybe paint a picture?

There are no limits to what you can imagine in your mind. Your imagination can change your world by making it a happier, brighter, more creative place to live.

Thank you for being you!

www.ingramcontent.com/pod-product-compliance
Lightning Source LLC
Chambersburg PA
CBHW061822290426
44110CB00027B/2949